Original title:
Tales from the Tallwoods

Copyright © 2025 Creative Arts Management OÜ
All rights reserved.

Author: Harrison Blake
ISBN HARDBACK: 978-1-80567-369-9
ISBN PAPERBACK: 978-1-80567-668-3

Memoirs of the Moths

Once flew in circles, lost in the glow,
A lamp was their party, putting on a show.
They danced and they darted, all a-flutter,
Until one bumped the bulb, what a loud mutter!

With wings all a-tickle from the bulb's bright heat,
They stumbled and tumbled, tripped on their feet.
'Oh dear,' said one moth, with a giggly sigh,
'Let's stick to the twilight, where the moon is nigh.'

The Harmony of Hushed Steps

In the quiet of night, while all creatures snooze,
A raccoon and a fox, sharing shoes of blues.
They tiptoed and giggled, trying to sneak,
Each step went a-crunch with a comical squeak.

The owl gave a hoot, tilting its head,
'You two are a circus, go back to your bed!'
But off they went laughing, under stars' bright cue,
A midnight parade of mischief, and goo!

The Chronicle of the Cuckoo

Cuckoo on duty, setting clocks at dawn,
With a wink and a chuckle, he stretched on the lawn.
His voice was a melody, a raucous delight,
Yet the twist was his timing—oh, what a sight!

A squirrel took notes, on a leaf made of bark,
'Let's see, that's cuckoo at three, it's a lark!'
But every time noon came, they'd hear a big 'Boo!'
The cuckoo just laughed, 'Time flies when it's true!'

The Lure of the Melodious Brook

By the babbling brook, where the fish love to tease,
   A frog in a bowler danced with the breeze.
   He croaked out a tune, oh what a delight,
   A chorus of giggles sparkled that night.

  The fish swam along, tapping tails in the flow,
  As water bugs tapped their tiny feet in a row.
  'Join in our song!' croaked the frog with a spin,
  But they all jumped so high, it was chaos akin!

Secrets Held in Root and Stone

In the woods, the trees do chatter,
Whispers shared, a little fatter.
Raccoons debate, the frogs all croak,
Over a leaf, their chuckles poke.

Underneath, the roots entwine,
Mice read novels, sipping brine.
Squirrels plot with nuts in tow,
While owls hoot the midnight show.

Rabbits rave about the moon,
Dancing lightly to a tune.
Tales of acorns tossed around,
With giggles echoing the ground.

Nature's jesters, wild and free,
Joking 'bout their next big spree.
In every nook and each small stone,
Secrets sprout where laughter's grown.

The Songbird's Wistful Cry

High above, the songbirds swoon,
Hoping to catch a silly tune.
With every flitter, every glide,
They weave tales of a feathered ride.

A robin claims to steal the show,
While mockingbirds steal lines they know.
Every chirp a joke in flight,
A raucous laugh from morning light.

A magpie's grin is wide and bright,
As he pirouettes in sheer delight.
With cheeky flair, he steals the scene,
Dancing, prancing, ever keen.

But then comes dusk, and oh, what luck!
A creaky branch, oh what a cluck!
As feathers flop and laughter swirls,
The songbirds stumble, laughter whirls.

Enigma of the Gnarled Branch

On a branch that twists and bends,
A wise old turtle claims he lends.
Fishy tales of winds that blow,
Squirrels giggle, "Oh no, no!"

There's a mystery in shadows cast,
Where gnarled limbs hold the past.
A cricket sits, a stand-up pro,
With punchlines that steal the show.

While owls hoot their nightly rant,
The bushes rustle, secrets chant.
Each snap of twig a punchline flung,
In the woods where all songs are sung.

With laughter stitched in every knurl,
Nature winks, a fun-filled whirl.
In the heart of this leafy mess,
Lies a humor that won't digress.

Fireflies in the Midnight Thicket

In thickets dark where fireflies shine,
They flash their lights, each blink divine.
Tiny jesters in the night,
Winking secrets, oh what a sight!

Hovering close, they whisper bold,
Of summer tales that never grow old.
Beetles join, in shuffle and spin,
Together they dance, let the fun begin!

A glow worm grins, "I lead the way!"
While crickets chirp, "Hip-hip-hooray!"
Each flicker like a joke well told,
Filling the thicket with marigold.

So in the hush, the laughter glows,
With every twinkle, the mischief grows.
In the midnight's playful embrace,
Fireflies waltz in a merry chase.

A Mosaic of Green and Gold

In a forest dressed in yellow,
The squirrels danced like jello,
With acorns flying through the air,
Chasing each other without a care.

The rabbit wore a tiny hat,
Sipped tea while sitting flat,
A hedgehog served the cake with glee,
While birds debated who's the bee.

Frogs performed a wild ballet,
Leaping high, come what may,
As chipmunks brought confetti rounds,
In a forest party full of sounds.

Laughter echoed through the leaves,
Where every creature weaves,
A story of fun and cheer,
In this woodland atmosphere.

The Caravan of the Wood Spirits

In twilight's glow, a merry band,
Of sprites and pixies, hand in hand,
With miniature carts of fruit and spice,
They roamed the woods, oh so nice.

One tripped over a sleeping gnome,
And landed right upon his comb,
The gnome awoke with quite a shout,
"That's not how you get about!"

A raccoon played the tambourine,
As owls hooted, what a scene!
The dancefloor made of twigs and leaves,
Where all the woodland friends believe.

With laughter bright, they spun around,
Where silliness and joy abound,
Each whispered secret, every wink,
In a playful world, they'd never sink.

Oaths of the Leafy Brood

Beneath the oaks, the young leaves swore,
To tickle roots and sing out more,
While acorns pledged to roll and play,
With smiles bright to greet the day.

The wind was caught up in a laugh,
As branches danced like a silly staff,
"Come join us on this leafy spree,"
A mushroom giggled, "You'll agree!"

Worms in hats wiggled with pride,
In their own parade, they did not hide,
And butterflies, a fluttering sight,
Joined in the chaos, oh what a night!

In the forest, the jokes were plenty,
With all the spirits feeling giddy,
Those leafy oaths, forever sworn,
In the whimsy of the early morn.

Whims of the Woodland Faery

A faery wished for shoes of leaves,
And tumbled down, oh what mischief weaves,
With every step, a little squish,
"Perhaps I'll stick to my old fish!"

In fields of clover, fun was found,
She painted faces all around,
With silly grins and wild styles,
And every creature laughed for miles.

Fireflies winked a guiding light,
While crickets played into the night,
The faery giggled, spun and twirled,\nCrafting joy in her little world.

So come, dear friends, don't be a fret,
Join in the whims; you won't regret,
In the woodland where laughter flies,
Underneath those starry skies.

Reverie in the Autumn Dew

Dew drops glimmer like tiny pearls,
In the morning light, nature swirls.
Squirrels chatter, doing a dance,
While rabbits hop, lost in a trance.

Crisp leaves crunch beneath tiny feet,
A raccoon pauses, too cute to beat.
The sun peeks in with a golden grin,
As the forest laughs, inviting joy in.

A breeze whispers jokes from the trees,
The branches sway, tickled with ease.
Nature's jesters, all in a row,
Spreading delight from below to the glow.

In the dewy morn, with mischief and cheer,
The woods come alive, laughter draws near.
So listen closely as spirits conspire,
In the playful woods, where joy won't tire.

The Spirit Beneath the Surface

Beneath the pond, where ripples play,
A frog croaks tales of the silliest day.
Fish tease him, darting with glee,
As dragonflies buzz, a wild jubilee.

The water's spirit takes a leap,
Belly flops that make you weep!
Giggling lily pads join in the fun,
As sunbeams dance, one by one.

With cheeky splashes, they plot a prank,
The ducklings quack as they swim in rank.
A frog slips and falls, what a sight,
Making ripples of laughter, pure delight!

The water looks on with a wink and a grin,
In the joyful depths, where the laughter begins.
So dive right in, embrace the absurd,
Join the merry spirit, every sound heard.

Insights from the Elder Tree

An old tree speaks in whispers low,
Stories of squirrels stealing the show.
With limbs outstretched, it chuckles wide,
As the woodland critters frolic inside.

They scamper up and down the trunk,
Finding mischief in every funk.
The acorns drop like tiny bombs,
As laughter erupts in playful qualms.

Roots twist secrets, ages untold,
The tree's wise humor never gets old.
With a bark so rough, yet heart so warm,
In its embrace, all troubles transform.

So, gather 'round for a laugh or two,
From the elder who knows just what to do.
Each creak and groan, a punchline given,
In the heart of the woods, joy is driven.

Sights and Sounds of the Forgotten Glade

In a glade where whispers barely roam,
The shyest critters have found a home.
A hedgehog rolls, with quite a flair,
As a shy deer watches from behind a pear.

Mushrooms giggle as the breezes tease,
While fireflies dance with graceful ease.
The shadows play tricks, a game on their own,
Creating shadows so humorously grown.

From tangled vines, the frogs serenade,
Making melodies under the shade.
With harmonies sweet, and beats so bold,
Even the trees sway, losing control.

But one sly fox with a whisker of wit,
Throws a joke that makes all spirits lift.
In the forgotten glade, where laughter's a breeze,
Every moment sparkles with friendly tease.

Through the Severed Vines

In the garden of giggles, where laughter entwines,
A squirrel stole my sandwich, oh how he dines!
Chasing him round the tree, what a sight to see,
   He dropped it for a nut; I guess it's just me.

The flowers were chuckling, petals in a dance,
While a hedgehog wore sunglasses, caught in a trance.
A caterpillar crawled, dreaming of the show,
   But slipped on a leaf, and fell flat below.

The sunbeam giggled, tickling my nose,
As the garden erupted in laughter, it glows.
With vines all around, in this jolly old place,
Every twist and turn brings a smile to my face.

So, if you wander this way, take heed of your loot,
For the critters around here will give you a root.
A frolicsome day in this whimsical land,
   Where jokes hang like fruit, easily at hand.

Gauntlets of Golden Dust

In a realm of odd trinkets, a box full of fun,
I found gauntlets of gold, shining bright like the sun.
When slipped on my hands, oh, what a delight!
They danced like crazy, day turned into night.

At first, I thought I'd be the hero, so grand,
But they just made me twirl and leap unplanned.
The cat looked bemused, tail high in the air,
As I pranced through the room, like I hadn't a care.

A dust cloud surrounded; it sparkled and spun,
As I tried to sweep up, but I just made it fun.
With every wild flail, I painted the walls,
A masterpiece crafted from giggles and brawls.

Eventually, they faded, quiet as a sigh,
Leaving me in laughter, under the blue sky.
So if you find a treasure covered in dust,
Beware of the joy, it might just combust!

The Heralds of Green Horizons

In the meadows of mirth, where the daisies do play,
The heralds of joy sing through every day.
Green frogs in bow ties, croak out a tune,
While butterflies twirl under the cheeky moon.

A snail with a trumpet claims the center stage,
He's wrinkled but charming, full of good age.
His notes carry softly, like whispers in breeze,
As the flowers sway gently, dancing with ease.

The bumblebees buzz in a jubilant hum,
They've gathered a band; oh, what have they done?
With a wiggle and jiggle, they cause quite a stir,
While ants tap their feet, all in a whir.

So come all ye wanderers, heed these merry leads,
Join the band of the odd with their whimsical deeds.
In the warmth of the sun, where the laughter ignites,
Every corner unveils whimsical delights.

Reflections on the Water's Edge

At the water's edge, where chuckles reside,
The ducks wear small glasses, with elegance and pride.
They waddle around, telling stories of old,
While the fish giggle softly, in scales made of gold.

A frog struck a pose, croaking jokes to the crowd,
As the reeds swayed along, like they were so proud.
A splash from a friend, turns laughter to glee,
And the ripples of joy reflect back at me.

The sun dipped low, painting the sky,
While a sneaky raccoon made a pie and then shy.
He slipped on a rock, with a plop and a splat,
Leaving us roaring, with laughter so fat.

So if you find yourself by this giggling stream,
Remember the laughter, and let out a beam.
In the giggle of water, where silliness reigns,
The memories we forge will dance in our brains.

Shadows of the Wandering Oak

In the shade of the great old tree,
Squirrels argue over acorns free.
One wears a hat that's far too grand,
While the other claims it's all just planned.

Rabbits tumble in a silly race,
While a wise old turtle finds his pace.
"I'm not slow, I'm just quite wise!"
He shouts, as he chuckles at their cries.

A crow caws loud, says, "Look at me!"
Dancing on branches, proud as can be.
But he trips on a twig, and oh what a sight,
Spreading his wings like a clumsy kite.

As shadows fade and laughter rings,
The woodland hums with joy it brings.
Under the oak, where fables grow,
Silly mischief, stealing the show!

Beneath the Verdant Veil

Underneath the leafy camo,
A raccoon sings and struts a sham-o.
His tail a banner, bold and bright,
He jigs about, a comical sight.

A hedgehog says, "I'm sharp and proud!"
While the little birds giggle, chirping loud.
"Prickly dance? Not quite my style!"
The hedgehog grins and stays awhile.

There's a deer who thinks she's quite a star,
Posing like a model, oh so bizarre!
But trips on a root, with a thud and a gasp,
She jumps up quickly, with pride to clasp.

In this green realm, laughter fills the air,
With every mishap, the forest shares.
Under the veil, where joy unfolds,
Nature's antics turn into gold!

The Enchanted Glade's Song

In a glade where the mushrooms sway,
A fairy fumbles in her play.
Her wand goes zap, then down she plops,
Whispers of laughter, never stops.

A gnome with a belly round and wide,
Offers mushrooms as his pride.
"Take a bite," he gives a cheer,
But ends up tasting too much beer!

Breezes blow through willow charms,
As frogs croak out in silly psalms.
They jump and flop with glee and fun,
Turning the glade into a run!

When night unveiled its twinkling lights,
The creatures join in playful flights.
In the enchanted glade, laughter's the key,
Where every mishap's a grand jubilee!

Chronicles of the Moonlit Grove

Under the moon's amused stare,
The owl tells tales with splendid flair.
"Did you hear of the raccoon's feast?
He danced with a fox, the silliest beast!"

A badger snoozes with dreams so wide,
Of cheese platters served on a silver tide.
But wakes to find, oh what a plight,
His visions gone; it was all a night!

The cricket sings in a funny tone,
While fireflies blink, like stars alone.
Each note a giggle, each spark a laugh,
As critters gather for a jolly half!

In this grove where moonbeams play,
Stories weave in a whimsical way.
Chronicles spun with a twist of delight,
Where laughter shadows the peaceful night!

The Keeper of the Whispering Trail

In the woods, where shadows dance,
A keeper laughs at every chance.
Squirrels gossip, then they flee,
With acorns tossed, wild and free.

He wears a hat that's far too grand,
And jokes that come from a merry band.
The bunnies roll in fits of glee,
As he tells tales of the tallest tree.

With twinkling eyes, he starts to prance,
Convinced he'll lead a woodland dance.
But tripping over roots, oh dear!
The laughter echoes far and near.

So every step along the trail,
Is filled with giggles, bright and frail.
The keeper chuckles, and so do we,
In this strange, silly jubilee.

Mesmerizing Murmurs of the Ferns

In a thicket, where the ferns are proud,
A secret party fills the crowd.
They whisper tunes, both sly and sweet,
Inviting all to take a seat.

A mouse in spectacles starts to croon,
While fireflies join with a bright tune.
The elder tree taps its feet with cheer,
As frogs in bow ties appear, oh dear!

With every rustle, laughter grows,
The ferns shake lightly, as humor flows.
A hedgehog juggles tiny stones,
And giggles spill in playful tones.

The night giggles with a playful stir,
As nature joins in a whimsical blur.
The murmurs weave a funny song,
In the ferns, where we all belong.

Frosted Dawn in Sylvan Silence

At dawn, the world wears frosty lace,
And squirrels leap with a comical grace.
In every flake of morning frost,
A giggle echoes, never lost.

The owls are sleepy, blinking slow,
While creatures plan a morning show.
A dance-off starts with quite a flair,
From hedgehogs prancing without a care.

In shimmering light, they stomp and twirl,
While snowflakes fall like a sparkling pearl.
The bunnies hop in mismatched socks,
Unfazed by winter's frosty knocks.

So raise a cup to dawn's bright grin,
Where laughter greets the day begin.
In sylvan silence, joy takes flight,
Frosted fun, oh what a sight!

Revelations at Dusk's Doorway

As the sun sinks low, the secrets twine,
Creatures gather, each one divine.
A wise old owl starts with a joke,
That makes the shadows giggle and soak.

The rabbits cackle, their ears in a flop,
While toads near the pond give a mighty hop.
"Knock, knock!" they cry, "Who's there, do you know?"
"Olive" responds a shy little crow.

With every chuckle, the dusk unfolds,
As stories of silliness start to mold.
A feast of laughter fills the air,
With every creature ready to share.

So as the daylight slips away,
The woods come alive in a funny play.
In the doorway of dusk, they spin and sway,
Turning the night into a grand cabaret.

Enigma of the Hidden Glades.

In secret corners, shadows play,
The trees gossip in a sprightly way.
A squirrel steals a baker's treat,
While mushrooms dance in tiny feet.

The brook giggles with a splash,
As frogs croak tunes in wild thrash.
A fox winks with a cunning grin,
While rabbits hop, their dance begins.

The flowers wear their colors bright,
Each one prancing, pure delight.
A raccoon wears a paper hat,
In this glade, all things are chat!

So come and join the merry cheer,
In every nook, there's fun near here.
With every rustle, every twist,
Hidden laughter you won't miss!

Whispers of Ancient Pines.

The pines are talking, oh so sly,
With rustles like a secret sigh.
An owl chuckles from its perch,
While crickets play a concert's lurch.

A squirrel juggles acorns high,
Beneath the branches they fly by.
Chipmunks giggle, tails a-twitch,
Laughing at the owl's small glitch.

The winds swirl tales of days gone by,
As branches sway, they flirt and pry.
A branch might snap, that's just their way,
To keep the forest jokes at play.

So listen close to whispers there,
In every breeze, a joke to share.
The ancient pines hold laughter neat,
In shadows where the wild things meet!

Echoes in the Canopy.

Up above, the branches sway,
With echoes of a child's play.
A parrot squawks a silly tune,
While fireflies dance like little moons.

The leaves are fluttering, full of cheer,
A giggling brook flows crystal clear.
A deer trips over a little vine,
As nature chuckles, oh so fine!

Beneath the canopy's winking light,
The shadows come to join the fight.
A raccoon makes a daring leap,
And stumbles down, not one soul weeps.

So watch the antics, big and small,
Each rustle echoes a forest ball.
In every nook, a whimsy beam,
Where laughter's woven into dream!

The Forest's Secret Keeper.

A secret keeper in the grove,
Wears wise old eyes and furry strobe.
With every rustle, tales unfold,
A wink, a grin, so feel the bold.

The mushrooms giggle with delight,
While sleepy owls take to flight.
A rabbit in a vest so small,
Pretends to read, yet starts to fall.

The leaves whisper with playful grace,
As breezy paths lead on a chase.
A chipmunk eats a snack divine,
While dancing 'round a crooked pine.

So wander through the forest wide,
Find friends and foes with nature's guide.
In every twist, a smile appears,
Where laughter drowns away our fears!

The Serpent's Lament

In the grass a serpent slithers,
Complaining loud for all to hear.
"Why do the rabbits hop so quick?"
"I'd join the dance, but I have no rear!"

With a wiggle and a hiss, he sighs,
"Oh, to have legs would be just grand!"
But with no feet, he only lies,
Dreaming of a Bambi band!"

So the critters gather round,
To share their laughs with scales and skin.
The serpent frowns, but joy is found,
As they dance and swirl in a spin!

He grumbles still, but can't resist,
A chuckle here and wink of eye.
"Perhaps a song's a better twist,
Than sulking low while others fly!"

Tales of the Starry Bough

High above, the branches sway,
Whispering secrets throughout the night.
A squirrel perched with dreams of play,
Yells, "Catch my acorn, if you might!"

But the owl hoots with wise old mirth,
"What do you think you are, my friend?
An acorn toss, of little worth,
While I sit here, all wise to lend!"

The raccoon joins with a sneaky grin,
"Let's have a game, and up with the stakes!
Loser must prance on the tree's thin skin,
While the other giggles, oh, the shakes!"

Round and round, the moon creeps high,
The tree stands firm with its leafy crown.
Each critter laughs beneath the sky,
As stories twinkle, far from town!

Parables of the Ancient Oak

Beneath the old and creaky oak,
A rabbit asks for wisdom fair.
"Oh, trusted tree, have you a joke?"
"Why did the chicken cross? I dare!"

The oak chuckles in slow delight,
"To get to the roots that help him grow!"
The forest joins in laughter bright,
Even the shyest hedgehog in tow!"

A fox arrives, with a twinkly gaze,
"Tell me a riddle to spark my mind!
What leaps through bushes, in nimble ways?"
"A hop, a skip, a playful bind!"

The lessons learned beneath the boughs,
Are knots of fun in the weathered bark.
Full of giggles and friendly vows,
As day drifts off into the dark!

Voices in the Wildwood

In deep wildwood, the echoes speak,
A bear with greed for all things sweet.
"I'll have my honey, I've got a beak!"
But all he finds is sassy feet!

The bees buzz back with stubborn pride,
"You can't just waddle in and take!
We've got a dance, come join the slide!"
"Who needs your honey? I'm on a break!"

Hares hop in with nimble toes,
"Just share the feast, and don't be tamed!
A berry's joy is free to those,
Who are not grumpy or too ashamed!"

So laughing, prancing, all in sync,
The wildwood chorus fills the air.
While bear looks on, not quite in pink,
And wonders why they share the fare!

Fables of the Ferny Dell

In the dell where ferns have grown,
A frog wore shoes, quite overblown.
He leaped and danced with such delight,
But tripped and fell, oh what a sight!

The rabbits laughed, they couldn't wait,
To see his antics, oh what fate!
With each fall, his shoes would squeak,
And in the mud, he'd take a peek.

A tortoise strolled, quite slow and proud,
Said, "Frog, you're foolish, don't be loud!"
But hopping high, that frog would say,
"Look at me! I rock this play!"

So in the ferny dell they stay,
With laughter brightening their day.
No worries here, just joy and fun,
In the dell where fables run.

Driftwood Dreams

By the shore, where driftwood lies,
A crab with dreams began to rise.
He built a castle, tall and grand,
With toothpicks stuck in seashell sand.

A seagull landed, laughed out loud,
"Your castle's small, you silly crowd!"
The crab replied, with a cheeky grin,
"It just needs tides to let it win!"

Then came the waves, they crashed and played,
And washed away what crab had made.
But he just chuckled, splashed around,
"Tomorrow, I'll build on firmer ground!"

So under the sun, soaked with glee,
The crab made driftwood dreams carefree.
With laughter mingling with the sea,
In his castle, he felt so free.

Soliloquies of the Stone Pine

In the grove, stood a stone pine,
With thoughts so deep, he'd sip on brine.
"I can be strong," he'd gently sigh,
"Or dance with leaves beneath the sky."

A squirrel paused, with acorn in hand,
"Your soliloquies are quite unplanned!
Why ponder so when you can play?
Just sway with breezes, come what may!"

The stone pine giggled, swayed a bit,
"I'll show you what this trunk can hit!
With each breeze that comes my way,
I'll twist and twirl to let you stay!"

So under stars, they shared their tales,
Of moonlit nights and wind-blown gales.
This stone pine's heart, forever true,
Brought joy to every creature, too!

The Flight of the Sable Hawk

A sable hawk, with feathers sleek,
Took flight with grace, a thrill to seek.
He soared through clouds, so high, so bold,
And spotted a fish, a sight to behold!

But as he dove with great finesse,
He missed the splash, what a mess!
With flapping wings, he circled back,
Declared, "I'm just testing my own knack!"

The elder owls, the wise brigade,
Chuckled softly, "He's quite the grade!
That hawk believes he's fit for kings,
But he's off pace when fishy flings!"

Yet flying high, with spirit free,
The sable hawk just laughed with glee.
For in his heart, he'd always know,
That every dive brings joy and show!

Legends Carved in Bark

Once a squirrel wore a tiny hat,
Claimed it made him wise as a cat.
He read the trees, or so he swore,
Only for birds to take it for decor.

A wise old owl thought he'd train
A rabbit to dance in the rain.
But the rabbit forgot his own feet,
And slipped on a beet, what a feat!

A raccoon tried to steal some shine,
With a clever plan and a straight line.
But instead of treasure, he found a shoe,
And now it's a prize at the raccoon zoo.

The leaping frogs held a grand parade,
In tutus, they danced, not knowing they played.
As the sun set low, they leapt with a cheer,
While beetles below rolled back in sheer fear.

Dances of the Twilight Spirits

In the dusk, the shadows sway,
Whispering secrets, come what may.
The fireflies twinkle, a bright shindig,
While the bushes sway like a wiggly pig.

Mice gossip about the party tunes,
Under the careful watch of the moon.
They spin and twirl, a chaotic ballet,
While owls chuckle at their nightly play.

Raccoons join in with a splash of pride,
Taking center stage, they salsa and glide.
While badgers hum a tune from afar,
Encouraging the dance of the evening star.

Laughter rings through the leafy halls,
As critters gather, enchanted by calls.
In the end, they toast with dewberry punch,
For tomorrow awaits a similar brunch.

The Lore of the Timbered Mantle

Once a tree had a claim to fame,
For hosting a family of wild game.
A porcupine thought it a fine trade,
Gave out stories, a huge charade.

With leaves as gold, the stories spun,
Of raccoons who wore hats made of sun.
Each tale grew tall as the timbered trees,
While deer snickered, "Oh please, oh please!"

The chipmunks held a debate at noon,
Arguing if the sun was a balloon.
But their voices rose, with vigor and cheer,
A woodpecker shrieked, "I'll sell your gear!"

Under the bark, secrets entwined,
In the laughter of creatures that intertwined.
Every whispered yarn and grin spread wide,
In the timbered mantle where whispers abide.

Dreams Upon the Mossy Carpet

Where the moss grows thick and green,
Creatures gather for the unseen.
Bunnies brag about their sprint,
While turtles move in a steady hint.

The frogs croon tales of midnight bites,
While crickets play their high-flying flights.
Each leaf is a stage for a concert grand,
As the fireflies direct, in a sparkly band.

Under the moon, the animals scheme,
With dreams as wild as a cloud's fluff beam.
A newfound joke leaves them all in places,
As laughter bounces to the hidden spaces.

Through the thicket, the stories twine,
On a carpet of moss, where the sun may shine.
With snickers and giggles, they settle down,
On this whimsical bed with no frowns to be found.

Whispers of the Ancient Grove

In the woods where the squirrels play,
The trees have tales they love to say.
A bear once danced on a sunny day,
And a rabbit wore bright shoes, hip-hip-hooray!

The owl wore glasses, just for show,
Claiming he sees better, oh what a pro!
The frogs croaked jokes in a high-pitched flow,
While the raccoon tried juggling, stealing the show.

A deer with a top hat strutted with flair,
While beavers held parties, making quite a pair.
The porcupines laughed, their quills in the air,
In this ancient grove, there's fun everywhere!

And so if you wander through leafy lanes,
Listen closely, you'll hear all their gains.
Nature's giggles tickle the brains,
In this merry grove, laughter never wanes!

Shadows Beneath the Canopy

Under the branches, all cozy and bright,
The shadows play games, oh what a delight!
A raccoon tried hiding, but oh what a sight,
With a stash of snacks, he got quite a fright.

The deer played tag with the nimble old fox,
While squirrels had races with acorn-filled socks.
The birds chirped tunes like fine music boxes,
And the rabbits cracked jokes while tying up locks.

The hedgehog wore sneakers, thought he was slick,
But stumbled on twigs, what a funny trick!
The turtles laughed slow, always taking their pick,
Beneath the tall trees, time's tick-tock is quick.

So join them now under the leafy expanse,
Where laughter is shared with each little prance.
In this shady realm, take your chance,
To giggle and wiggle, join in the dance!

Secrets of the Verdant Realm

In the realm where the ferns and flowers bloom,
A chipmunk wore shades, claiming 'I need more room!'
He danced with a snail, beneath the full moon,
While a lazy old cat hummed a sleepy tune.

The hedgehogs baked pies, not a single one burnt,
A chef in the woods, oh how they all yearned!
The squirrels made salad—didn't know how to turn,
But with every big laugh, their humor returned.

The buzzing bees held a raucous debate,
About the best honey and proper garden plate.
The rabbits brought carrots, served on a crate,
In this verdant realm, all was first-rate!

Follow the laughter through meadow and glade,
Where each silly secret is joyfully laid.
In this whimsical world, let worries be swayed,
And bask in the fun that the forest has made!

Echoes of the Evergreen

In the heart of the forest, where pine needles sway,
Lies a hedgehog named Henry who loves to play.
He challenges raccoons to races each day,
While the owls hoot loudly, hip-hip-hooray!

A wise old porcupine told a tall tale,
Of chasing a fox while riding a whale.
The laughter erupted, like wind in a gale,
While the beavers built boats made entirely of kale.

There's a mouse in a hat, who thinks he's a prince,
With jokes and antics that never grow dense.
And a crow swaps stories, makes puns with a whince,
Echoing giggles, the forest's fine fence.

So wander through woodlands, where joy is the theme,
Where laughter is sparkling, like sun on a stream.
In this evergreen land, life's but a dream,
Full of funny antics that make the heart beam!

The Veil Between Worlds

In a forest where whispers play,
Squirrels chat in a grand ballet,
The mushrooms giggle, the trees conspire,
As branches tickle a hedgehog's attire.

A rabbit wearing a fancy hat,
Sips tea with a very chatty cat,
They plot schemes to confuse the lark,
Who thinks he's the king—a quirk so stark!

On windy days, they dance with glee,
Chasing shadows like a lost bumblebee,
The veil between realms is a jolly grin,
Where even the grumpiest badger joins in!

With tales spun in this lively wood,
Every giggle, every friendly hood,
A world where laughter is the best spell,
In the antics of woods, all's truly well!

The Twilight's Promise

As twilight curls in hues of peach,
The owls and the frogs exchange their speech,
A raccoon juggles acorns with flair,
While a wise old turtle just winks and stares.

The stars peek down with a knowing smile,
Two fireflies race, oh, what a fun trial!
In the background, the crickets play tag,
While a sleepy fox drags a quilted rag.

Though shadows creep, no one feels fear,
For laughter echoes, and spirits are clear,
In the night, mischief brews in the air,
As giggles burst wild like a breath of fresh dare!

So here in the twilight, let mirth remain,
Where folly dances on the sweet refrain,
With a promise of joy that never shall wane,
In the woods where the hearts are always untamed!

Solace of the Shaded Haven

In the shaded haven, mischief brews,
Where shadows giggle and gossip ensues,
A parrot teaching a goat to sing,
While a sunbeam dances, doing its thing.

The ants throw parties under a leaf,
While a chipmunk raves, seeking some chief,
A spider spins yarns of the wildest sort,
As grasshoppers leap, planning a sport.

Beneath the boughs, a chatty snail,
Recounts his travels without fail,
He claims to have race with the swiftest hare,
While everyone giggles, saying, "Oh, how rare!"

So here in the shade, joy's woven tight,
With friendships blooming in the soft twilight,
Every creature laughs at the wildest plot,
In this haven of mischief, joy's never forgot!

Secrets Weaving Through Roots

In the tangled roots where secrets lie,
Mice whisper tales as they scamper by,
A gopher knits during the sunset glow,
While the wise old owl says, "Don't tell, though!"

Caterpillars hold a fashion parade,
While beetles critique in a friendly charade,
A chatty crow caws, 'Secrets are fun!'
With mischief lurking in each setting sun!

The elder trees lean in to hear,
As whispers turn into giggles near,
A dance of roots with rhythmic shuffles,
Where even the stoic tall deer snuffles.

So glide through the woods with a bob and weave,
For in the quirks of nature, you won't believe,
As those secrets weave through roots so deep,
In a world of laughter, the heart takes a leap!

The Lorekeeper's Secret

In the woods where whispers dwell,
The lorekeeper tells a tale so swell.
With a wink and a chuckle, he spins quite a yarn,
Of squirrels that dance and a mischievous barn.

He claims that the trees all gossip and talk,
Trading secrets with every passing flock.
But who would believe a twig in a hat?
Just the raccoons who laugh, how about that!

The mushrooms prance and the bushes get bold,
As the stories unravel, a sight to behold.
They giggle and wiggle in the dappled light,
Under the moon's mischievous delight.

So next time you're walking past trunks so grand,
Listen closely, join the woodland band.
For the lorekeeper's secret is waiting for you,
In the tall, funny tales that the forest can brew.

Lost Songs of the Timberline

At the timberline, where the treetops sway,
The birds have forgotten the notes of their play.
With a flutter and flail, they try to recall,
But the tunes turn to giggles, cascading like fall.

The owls hoot how funny the chorus has become,
While the rabbits hop along, feeling quite numb.
A squirrel steals a note, with a flick of its tail,
And suddenly, all join the hilarious trail.

From the boughs of the pine, a melody floats,
It's a mix of old laughter and croaking of goats.
The harmony sways, a whimsical spree,
In a world where the melodies dance wild and free.

So gather your friends, let's sing our own tune,
In the quirky timberline beneath the full moon.
For the lost songs are back, with a twist of delight,
As the woods come alive in the magical night.

The Oak's Companions

Underneath the grand oak, friends gather 'round,
The company's lively, there's laughter abound.
With a wise old crow cracking jokes from above,
And a turtle who's slow, but shares tales of love.

The acorns drop down with a soft little thud,
As the fox offers snacks, a feast and some mud.
From morning till night, they share every scheme,
With giggles and grumbles, the best of the team.

While the sun sets low, they dance in a ring,
With fireflies winking, oh, what joy they bring!
The oak shakes with laughter, its branches all sway,
For friends are the treasures that brighten the day.

So join in the fun, don't be shy or coy,
In the shade of the oak, find your heart full of joy.
For companions in laughter make every tale bright,
By the old noble oak, in the warm soft twilight.

Lullabies of the Nightingale

In the dark of the night, a nightingale sings,
With melodies bubbling, as if he has wings.
His lullabies wrap like a soft, cozy quilt,
While the moon peeks in, showing joy that is built.

The crickets join in with a cheeky refrain,
With beats that make bunnies hop round in vain.
And the stars giggle softly, twinkling so bright,
As they dance with the moon in the heart of the night.

With a hop and a giggle, the critters all sway,
To the nightingale's tune, in a playful ballet.
A tapestry woven with joy and delight,
As the forest joins in, a musical flight.

So when shadows are long, and the world dims its light,
Listen close for the laughter, beneath the soft night.
For the lullabies carry a gift so divine,
In the heart of the woods, where the stars intertwine.

The Song of the Whispering Pines

In the forest where squirrels dance,
A pine tree whispers, it takes a chance.
"Cat up a tree? Oh what a sight!"
Their giggles echo, a pure delight.

Raccoons plotting midnight snacks,
Chattering loudly as they relax.
"Did you hear? The owls hoot loud!"
Their chatter flows, they're feeling proud.

A fox with style, sporting a hat,
Claims he's the coolest, just like a cat.
But the bunnies laugh, with twitching ears,
Oh what a show, it brings them cheers.

As leaves sway gently, the sun peeks through,
Nature's comedy, a playful view.
With pine trees singing in playful tones,
The forest thrives, a land of clones.

Mysteries in the Mist

Fog rolls in, a blanket of gray,
Mice in coats shuffle, in disarray.
"Where's our cheese?" one squeaks with dread,
While others trip over paths they've tread.

A deer wears glasses, reads a map,
She's lost, oh dear, and takes a nap.
"I had it earlier, I swear it's true!"
The trees just chuckle at the sight anew.

Misty shapes twist, start to appear,
A ghostly raccoon sipping on beer.
"I'm not a phantom!" he shouts in fright,
The forest roars, they giggle at night.

But as the sun breaks through the gloom,
The laughter swells, dispelling the doom.
Mysterious fun, in shadows they play,
The mist will lift, but laughter will stay.

Guardians of the Sylvan Heart

The squirrels band, with capes of green,
Guardians proud, a sight unseen.
"Watch out for acorns, they'll hit your head!"
They laugh in clusters, filling their shed.

A turtle slowly, with glasses so round,
Joins the crew, with wisdom profound.
"Slow and steady wins the race!"
But the rabbits zoom, just in chase.

The owls chuckle from branches high,
"Look at those fools, they're buzzing by!"
Who knew such chaos could be so grand?
In this wild kingdom, it's always planned.

Each critter knows their quirky role,
With silly antics, they reach the goal.
Together they guard their vibrant home,
In a world of humor, forever they roam.

Legends Beneath the Branches

Under the branches, whispers abound,
Legends of mischief, joyful sound.
"Once a frog danced, so fancy and spry!"
The others chortle, it's a funny lie.

A raccoon once stole a picnic basket,
Turning it over to cause a ruckus.
"Oops, my bad! I thought it was mine!"
Now he's the king, of snack time divine.

A tree stump holds the elder tales,
Of dancing critters and windy gales.
"Watch your step, or you might just fall!"
They gleefully shout, with humor for all.

Beneath the branches, stories flow,
Of laughter and joy, that all animals know.
In the heart of the woods, laughter does sing,
Forever together, in a whimsical spring.

Harmony in the Cedar's Fold

In the grove of trees so tall,
A squirrel danced, he had a ball.
Singing songs of acorn bliss,
While rabbits joined in with a kiss.

On a branch, a crow cawed loud,
Claiming space, so very proud.
But the fox just rolled his eyes,
And sent a wink to passing flies.

A turtle tried to join the fun,
But his slow pace was never done.
With a plop, he landed near,
And laughed so hard, he shed a tear.

All around was laughter shared,
In the woods, nobody dared.
To take it serious or be shy,
When the tallwoods sang a lullaby.

Forest Dreams in Starlit Nights

Underneath the moon's bright gaze,
Owl told stories in a haze.
He spun yarns of mishaps grand,
Like the chipmunk's silly band.

Raccoons wore hats, they pranced about,
Argued fiercely, but all in doubt.
The hedgehog rolled to steal a show,
With a dance that made them go, 'Whoa!'

A firefly sparkled, twinkling bright,
Guiding friends through the starry night.
With laughter echoing through the trees,
Even crickets hummed in harmony.

As dawn broke and dreams took flight,
They'd share their tales till morning light.
In the forest, where quirks align,
Every night blooms with pure design.

Scents of the Elderflower

The flowers bloomed, a fragrant delight,
Bees bustled in with all their might.
A dragonfly zoomed past with flair,
Showing off like he didn't care.

The skunk sneezed, what a funny sound,
Sending petals flipping round and round.
While the mice made a picnic spread,
With crumbs and giggles, sweetly fed.

A dandelion, brave and bold,
Challenged all, a sight to behold.
The sunflower just shook its head,
"Try again when you're not misled!"

Laughter echoed through the grove,
As all creatures danced and strove.
To find the scent of joy so pure,
In elderflower, they felt secure.

The Brooding Fault of the Bough

A branch fell down with a big ol' thud,
The wise old tree feared it was a flood.
But it only landed on a lazy cat,
Who snuggled up, like, 'What's up with that?'

Balancing acts of ants on high,
Stirred up chaos, oh me, oh my!
While the bear tripped over his own two paws,
And wondered suddenly, "What's the cause?"

The woodpecker laughed from above,
Seeing friends in clumsy love.
Even mushrooms joined in the show,
Popping up like, "Hey! Look at me go!"

In the greenwood, life's a circus bright,
Where every blunder brings delight.
With giggles shared beneath the bough,
All nature whispers, "Take a bow!"

Oaths in the Shade of Foliage

Under the leaves, a squirrel flipped,
With acorn plans that quietly slipped.
He whispered secrets to the breeze,
While ants held meetings under trees.

A worm in the dirt piped up with glee,
"I swear on my dirt, it's all just tea!"
The wise old owl rolled his big eyes round,
"You braggarts! Give us a break, abound!"

Laughter spilled from branches up high,
As the chipmunks joined, oh my, oh my!
Their oaths of mischief tickled the air,
In the shade where the forest went fair.

And all vowed to keep such nonsense near,
In that leafy realm where joy was dear.
With a wink and a twitch, they held their ground,
In oaths of silliness all around.

The Antiphon of Crickets

In the night, crickets held a show,
With chirps that danced just like a pro.
They sang of games and moonlit dreams,
Spinning tall stories, or so it seems.

One cricket claimed he flew to the stars,
While another boasted of racing cars.
A grasshopper chimed, with a ribbiting laugh,
"All of this chatter is just a gaffe!"

The night air buzzed with notes so spry,
As they debated the best apple pie.
The fireflies flickered, joining their fry,
A symphony bright under a starlit sky.

But in the morning, with daylight's toil,
The songs all faded, lost in the soil.
Yet the laughter lingered, sweet and spry,
In the echoes of crickets who aimed for the sky.

Scribblings in the Forest Floor

Amidst the roots, a raccoon sat,
With curious scribblings and a top hat.
"Look at my scroll!" he proudly declared,
As mushrooms giggled, unprepared.

A ladybug perched upon the grass,
"You think you're great, but you're just a class!
Your scribbles look like a child's own art,
But I wear my charm like the queen of the heart!"

The raccoon rolled his eyes with flair,
"My drawings are deep, they go everywhere!"
And then he drew a picture quite wild,
Of a dancing tree that just grinned and smiled.

The forest chuckled, the trees gave a spin,
In the most quirky world, they'd all fit in.
For every creature has their own score,
In the artful chaos upon the forest floor.

The Transformation of Silhouettes

As dusk did settle, shadows arrived,
A parade of forms, all bright and jived.
Each silhouette took up its own stance,
In a dark ballet, they dared to dance.

A bunny turned into a flickering ghost,
While a deer became a waiter, proud and engrossed.
A bush tree transformed into a grand chair,
Where frogs held court without a care!

The moonlight giggled, casting its glow,
As cats tiptoed in with a jazzy flow.
They tangoed and twirled, boldly afloat,
While crickets conducted on a tiny boat.

Then came the dawn, the magic withdrew,
And all returned to what we once knew.
But in the whispers of leaves that day,
The silhouettes promised to come out and play.

The Heartbeat of Dappled Light

In the woods where shadows play,
A squirrel cracked a joke today,
With acorns bouncing off a tree,
Laughter echoed, wild and free.

The sun peeked through leaves so bright,
Tickling branches, pure delight,
A rabbit danced, tripped on a root,
Even the mushrooms started to hoot!

Bees buzzed in their little choir,
Hearts of flowers filled with fire,
While owls tried to keep their cool,
But ended up a giggling fool.

The heart of the forest sings so sweet,
With every creature tapping a beat,
In this merry, vibrant place,
Joy dances in every space.

The Chronicles of the Wandering Trail

A fox with shoes too big to wear,
Stumbled down the path with flair,
He waved to a bear who waved right back,
And both just laughed at the silly track.

The path twisted like a curly fry,
With giggles floating up to the sky,
A turtle raced in its slow, proud way,
While birds cheered on from the golden hay.

There were whispers from the trees so tall,
That shared secrets of a great, big fall,
A raccoon fell flat after chasing a bee,
While frogs croaked tunes, full of glee.

This wandering trail never lets you be sad,
With every step, you're sure to be glad,
For in each turn and every bend,
You'll find laughter new around each friend.

Starlit Canopies and Their Secrets

Underneath the twinkling night,
A raccoon donned a hat so bright,
He claimed he found it from a star,
And danced like he was a rockstar!

The owls hooted silly rhymes,
Creating echoes, giggling chimes,
While fireflies joined the sparkling show,
Making the dark ground all aglow.

A frog with a crown croaked a tune,
Claiming he'd swoon under the moon,
And the trees swayed in a gentle breeze,
Whispering secrets with such ease.

These starlit canopies hold such charms,
Where every critter wraps in warm arms,
With laughter and tales of silly nights,
It's a world of joy that ignites.

The Untold Stories of Hollow Trees

Within the frame of an ancient oak,
Lies a squirrel who loves to joke,
He tells of adventures with nuts galore,
While the passing rabbit begs for more!

Each hollow bears tales of glee,
With whispers shared among the spree,
A hedgehog spins yarns of great delight,
Of moonlit dances on a whimsy night.

The wind carries laughter through the leaves,
While tree trunks dance as nature weaves,
A woodpecker's tap becomes a beat,
As creatures gather for a fun retreat.

The stories spoken, though often absurd,
Are cherished by all, hence, never blurred,
In these hollow homes where joy convenes,
Laughter sprouts amidst the greens.

Murmurs of the Maple Wood

In the woods, a squirrel danced,
With acorns stashed, he took a chance.
He tripped on roots, oh what a scene,
The giggles echoed, bright and keen.

A rabbit wore a tiny hat,
While ducks all quacked and shared a chat.
A porcupine tried to join the fun,
But he got stuck, oh what a run!

Every creature had their say,
In this wood, they laughed all day.
With joyful noise that filled the air,
You'd think they'd not a single care!

As night approached, they said, "Oh dear!",
"We'll tell our tales, let's gather near!"
The owls hooted, and fireflies winked,
In Maple Wood, they laughed and blinked.

Journeys through the Twisted Roots

A raccoon rode a snail in style,
Through tangled roots, they made a mile.
The snail complained, "This is too slow!"
The raccoon laughed, "Well, let's just go!"

With every twist, more friends appeared,
A frog declared, "I've persevered!"
Then one small mouse did trip and fall,
The wild root's loop made him so small!

But onward still, they made their way,
Past hidden jokes in shades of gray.
A tortoise joined with a wise old grin,
"I'll win the race," he said, "Just wait and spin!"

They found a field where laughter bloomed,
Each twist and turn, the fun resumed!
In nature's maze, they'd never tire,
With giggles sparking like a fire!

The Enchanted Hollow

In the hollow, a breeze whistled low,
Where mistletoe jumped like a yo-yo.
A gnome rode a snail, proud and able,
While fairies danced upon a table.

A toad sat croaking, telling tales,
Of how he once outsmarted snails.
He wore a crown made of dandelions,
While pixies giggled, breaking their silence.

Then squirrels with hats joined the cheer,
A wild parade began to appear.
With all their quirks and silly style,
Laughter bounced, stretching each mile!

As night fell down, they lit a fire,
While shadows danced, lifting their choir.
In the hollow, joy found a home,
Where whimsy thrived, and spirits roamed.

Sagas of the Wildflower Meadow

In the meadow where flowers spun,
A bee lost track of all his fun.
He buzzed around, full of glee,
But bumped his head on a honey tree!

A horsefly joked, "Now that's a sting!"
While butterflies all started to sing.
"Your buzz is funny, can't you see?"
The flowers giggled, "Join our spree!"

With colors dancing in the sun,
The wildflower gang just laughed and ran.
They'd spin and twirl, each bloom a star,
Creating laughter, near and far!

Each very odd blossom had a name,
Like Silly Sally, oh what a game!
In the meadow, fun found its place,
Where every petal wore a smiley face!

The Tapestry of Shadows

In the woods where shadows play,
The squirrels dance in a merry fray,
They tell jokes in nutty terms,
While owls hoot, yes, it confirms.

A raccoon claims he's quite the chef,
With acorn soufflé, he's quite adept!
But when he tastes, he makes a face,
Oh dear! A gooey nutty grace.

The rabbits giggle, their whiskers twitch,
As they pull pranks, oh what a hitch!
One found a shoe, a lost delight,
Now it's a hat, oh what a sight!

With shadows wrestling day and night,
The tallwoods buzz with pure delight,
A tapestry woven of laughter bright,
In every nook, a silly sight.

Legends Written in Leaves

In leaves, the legends softly sway,
They whisper tales of an odd ballet,
A hedgehog waltzing with a broom,
While foxes giggle, oh what a bloom!

The wise old trees nod with glee,
As squirrels share tales of victory,
One climbed so high, nearly to space,
But slipped on acorns—what a disgrace!

The fox writes songs in the air,
Of dandelions dancing without care,
His audience roars with laughter loud,
For even the bees can't form a crowd!

Legends twisted in nature's ink,
Each little critter on the brink,
Of giggles echoing through the leaves,
Where nonsense reigns, the heart believes.

Songs of the Seasoned Bark

On seasoned bark, the stories stain,
Of wise old snails who dodge the rain,
They sing of travels, slow but grand,
With every inch, a foreign land.

The mischievous vines, they intertwine,
Creating tunes of a wobbly line,
A pigeon hops on a floating log,
And claims he's king, a playful rogue!

The chipmunks hum in perfect time,
As frogs join in with a croaky rhyme,
Together they share a giggling spree,
Of tuneful tales, bright as can be.

With every note, the tallwoods cheer,
In harmony, they banish fear,
For the songs of bark, oh what a mark,
In forest halls, they dance till dark.

Enchanted Paths and Twirling Leaves

On enchanted paths, the leaves do twirl,
With prancing rabbits, oh what a whirl!
They skip and hop with tiny leaps,
A dance that tickles and never sleeps.

The mushrooms giggle under the sun,
As hedgehogs race, oh, what fun!
But tripping over their own little feet,
They tumble down, a clumsy feat!

The paths are lined with flowers bright,
Sprinkled with fairy dust, pure delight,
The bees buzz jokes in a merry round,
While butterflies swirl without a sound.

With every twist and turn they take,
The forest shivers, the trees all shake,
For enchanted paths and leaves that play,
Make every moment a funny day.

Twirling Leaves and Laughing Trees

Twirling leaves in a dizzy dance,
The tallwoods giggle, given a chance,
The wind joins in with a playful blow,
Spreading laughter wherever they go.

The trees stand tall, with bark so wise,
They throw their hands up to the skies,
As pinecones fall like funny hats,
Landing on heads of curious cats!

The playful breeze makes shadows chase,
While critters race in a nutty race,
One little chipmunk steals the show,
With acorn juggling, a real pro!

In the heart of the tallwoods, fun abounds,
Where laughter echoes in giggly sounds,
A world so bright, with charms to please,
Twirling leaves and laughing trees.

Canopies of Moonlight

Under the bright and watchful moon,
Squirrels dance to a jaunty tune.
Acorns roll like marbles down,
As owls hoot jokes that wear a crown.

Pine trees stretch in silly poses,
While bushes blush with fragrant roses.
The night is filled with laughter and glee,
As raccoons debate who stole the key.

Fairies giggle in sparkling light,
As fireflies flash, a charming sight.
They throw a party, wild and free,
For all the critters beneath the tree.

The moonbeams serve as the stage's light,
With shadows prancing, oh what a sight!
In canopies lush, the fun rolls on,
While the forest laughs until the dawn.

Growth Rings of Time

In the heart of woods, where secrets grow,
Old trees chuckle, claiming what they know.
Each ring tells stories, wild and absurd,
Of chipmunk thieves and gossiping birds.

A tree once tried to wear a hat,
But it was too big, imagine that!
Stuck on branches, it danced with flair,
As the forest laughed, don't you dare stare!

Bark beetles discuss the wood's old fate,
While roots hide tales of a mud pie date.
A bear once tripped in a race with a hare,
And both tumbled down, without a care.

Once in a while, the trees will sigh,
Sharing little secrets that make time fly.
With each ring, they laugh at their past,
The wisdom of woods, forever vast.

The Lore of the Lost Trail

On a trail that wiggles, twists, and bends,
A raccoon wanders, seeking his friends.
With a snack in hand, he calls out loud,
But all he finds is a sleepy cloud.

The sun shines bright, but shadows play,
As a lost shoe giggles and rolls away.
Where do lost things go when they're shy?
They play hide and seek 'til they fly high!

A frog croaks wisdom, holding court,
With a crown made of leaves, what a sport!
While the snails race at their snail-pace speed,
Claiming they'll win, but it's all just greed.

So if you wander and lose your way,
Just follow the giggles, let them sway.
The trail may twist, but don't feel blue,
For in the woods, there's always a crew!

Fleeting Glimmers in the Underbrush

In the underbrush, where glimmers hide,
A hedgehog spins, full of quirky pride.
He shows off moves with a twist and a shout,
While critters watch, they can't help but pout.

A beetle boasts of its shiny shell,
Telling tall tales, oh can you tell?
"I am the king of this grassy glade,
With my royal gold, I am never afraid!"

But faeries laugh, sprinkling dust,
Turning the brave to mere whims of rust.
They flit and flutter, creating delight,
While the hedgehog tumbles, what a sight!

In fleeting moments, laughter's reborn,
As trees whisper secrets, tell tales of scorn.
Amongst the green, life spins unrestrained,
In the underbrush, joy's never waned.

Chronicles in the Forest's Embrace

Once a squirrel wore a tie,
Chasing acorns all so spry.
He slipped and fell, a flurry,
Now he's the town's great story.

A wise old owl lost his shoe,
He hopped around, oh what a view!
The rabbits laughed in pure delight,
'Best-dressed bird, what a sight!'

A bear tried dancing with a moose,
They tangled up, what a funny ruse!
With giggles echoing through the trees,
Nature's laughter on the breeze.

A fox who fancied himself the king,
Wore a crown made of chicken wing.
His royal court, a bunch of crows,
All they want, a snack that glows!

Dances of the Willows

Under the willows, frogs compete,
For the best tap dance on their feet.
They twirl and leap with joyful cheers,
Making ripples, spreading glee for years.

A raccoon juggles berries and mud,
While a deer watches, shaking his thud.
With every slip, there's quite the scene,
Nature's circus, a sight to glean.

Bees buzzing in a wild ballet,
Spinning round on a sunny day.
They forgot the rhythm, lost their way,
And now they just buzz in disarray!

A turtle twirls, though he's quite slow,
With a hat made of grass, putting on a show.
His friends cheer loud, their voices combined,
In the forest dance, all worries unwind.

The Hidden Path in the Thicket

In the thicket, where secrets lay,
A hedgehog sings, but oh, what a stray!
His quills stuck in a twirling vine,
Complains, 'Is this a fashion design?'

A mouse on a bike zoomed down the way,
Curious eyes followed his sway.
He hit a bump, flew like a bird,
Squeaking, 'I should not have heard!'

The bushes giggled, the flowers sneezed,
As a clumsy raccoon searched for peas.
With every trip and tumble unmatched,
His dinner plans all were dispatched.

A fox gave his map a flip,
But it led to a nearby dip.
He found a pond, announced with glee,
'In the thicket, it's all about spree!'

Enigmas of the Twilight Glade

In the glade where shadows dance,
A frog wore goggles, took a chance.
He leapt and hopped, made quite a splash,
Claimed, 'I'm the prince, with style and dash!'

A firefly lit up like a star,
In the dark, he wasn't very far.
He tripped on roots, confused the glow,
Said, 'I'll stick to disco, you know?'

A hedgehog tried to pull a prank,
With a balloon tied to a plank.
He floated high, then fell with a thud,
And laughed, 'Well, that was quite the flood!'

A wise old tree shared a riddle,
'Why did the cat sit in the middle?'
All pondered hard, confusion spread,
'To catch the mouse, or join the fed?'

The Dance of Dappled Sunlight

In the clearing, shadows prance,
Squirrels twirl in a nutty dance.
Leaves giggle with a gentle sway,
Winking sunlight, come out to play.

Breezes whisper silly tunes,
While rabbits hop beneath bright moons.
Frogs perform a funny show,
As fireflies join, all aglow.

Nurtured by Nature

Down by the brook, frogs plot and scheme,
To catch the fish that slip like dream.
Bees bumble in a quest for sweet,
Planting giggles with every beat.

Mushrooms wear hats, all striped and bright,
To host a party in soft moonlight.
Raccoons wear masks, oh what a sight,
Planning mischief 'til the morning light.

The Lament of the Old Stone

An old stone sits with stories untold,
Mossy and wise, but feeling quite cold.
Crying out, 'Oh, where did they go?
The friends I had, all in a row!'

Birds chirp softly, sharing their snacks,
'Old buddy stone, lighten your cracks!'
With chuckles around, the stone does agree,
It finds joy in their company.

Cadence in the Forest Breeze

The forest sways with a breezy tune,
As creatures dance under the watchful moon.
A hedgehog twirls with a tiny flair,
While owls hoot, trying to share.

Squirrels chase tales that make them hiss,
A chipmunk nearly tumbles in bliss.
The rhythm flows, all hearts are light,
In this funny forest, wonder ignites.

The Hidden Edges of Wilderness

In the woods where laughter grows,
A squirrel juggles nuts in rows.
Wobbly owls on festive nights,
Bouncing on their branchy flights.

Foxes playing hide and seek,
Their sneaky giggles make me peek.
A bear in boots, oh what a sight,
Dancing under the moonlight!

Fables from the Elderwood Realm

Once a rabbit with a hat,
Claimed he could outsmart a cat.
They raced around the ancient tree,
But tripped on roots—both fell with glee.

A turtle told a tall, tall tale,
While playing cards with a white-tailed snail.
The cards went flying, what a mess,
Laughter echoed through the forest!

Guardians of the Timberline

The porcupine guards with prickly pride,
While chipmunks cheer and dance beside.
They hold a party, wild and loud,
With woodland critters, all so proud.

A raccoon wearing shades of gold,
Tells stories that never get old.
His friends all groan but can't resist,
They laugh and cheer, it's hard to miss!

Reflections in a Stillwood Pool

In a pond where frogs wear crowns,
They play their music, hopping round.
A fish with fins of rainbow hues,
Claims he's the best of all the blues.

The lilies giggle, swaying slow,
As ducklings parade in a single row.
A turtle floats, just takes it easy,
While all of nature feels quite breezy.

www.ingramcontent.com/pod-product-compliance
Lightning Source LLC
Chambersburg PA
CBHW051651160426
43209CB00004B/877